Alfred's Basic Piano Library

Popular Hits Complete Level 1

For the Later Beginner

Arranged by Tom Gerou

This series offers Broadway, pop, and movie music arrangements to be used as supplementary pieces for students. Soon after beginning piano study, students can play attractive versions of favorite classics, as well as the best-known popular music of today.

This book is correlated page-by-page with Lesson Book, Complete Level 1 of *Alfred's Basic Piano Library*; pieces should be assigned based on the instructions in the upper-right corner of each title page of *Popular Hits.* Since the melodies and rhythms of popular music do not always lend themselves to precise grading, you may find that these pieces are sometimes a little longer and more difficult than the corresponding pages in the Lesson Book. The teacher's judgment is the most important factor in deciding when to assign each arrangement.

When the books in the *Popular Hits* series are assigned in conjunction with the Lesson Books, these appealing pieces reinforce new concepts as they are introduced. In addition, the motivation the music provides could not be better. The emotional satisfaction that students receive from mastering each song increases their enthusiasm to begin the next one.

Produced by
Alfred Music
P.O. Box 10003
Van Nuys, CA 91410-0003
alfred.com

ISBN-10: 1-4706-3384-1
ISBN-13: 978-1-4706-3384-4

Cover Photos: Music speakers: © Shutterstock.com / Martin M303 • Headphones: © Shutterstock.com / Jiri Hera

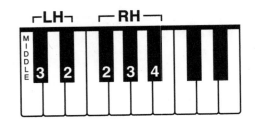

Use with Alfred's Basic Piano Library,
Lesson Book, Complete Level 1,
after page 7.

Minecraft

(from *Minecraft*)

FOR BLACK KEY GROUPS ABOVE MIDDLE

Composed by Daniel Rosenfeld
Arr. by Tom Gerou

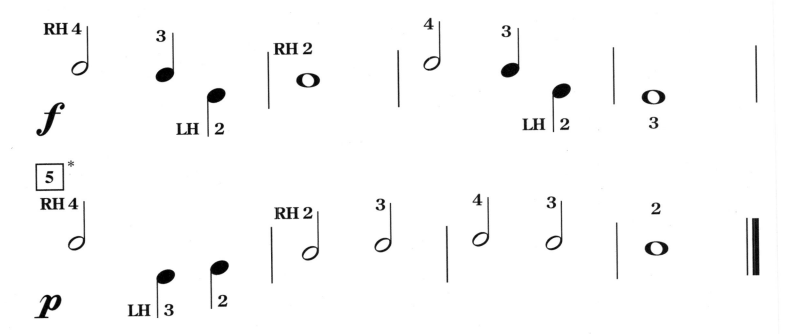

*measure number

DUET PART (Student plays 1 octave higher.)

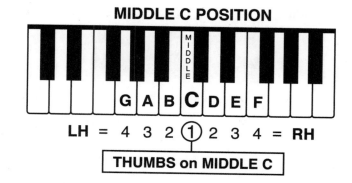

Iron Man

(from *Iron Man*)

Words and Music by Frank Iommi, John Osbourne,
William Ward and Terence Butler
Arr. by Tom Gerou

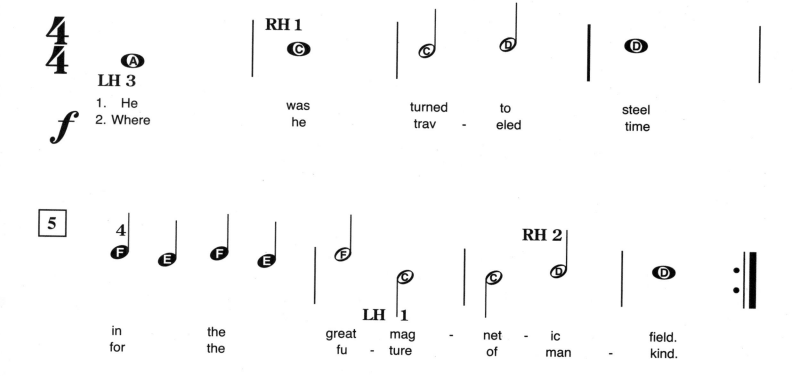

DUET PART (Student plays 1 octave higher.)

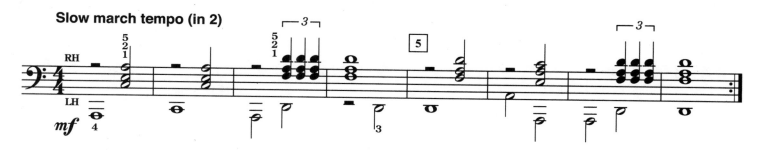

Use after page 11.

4

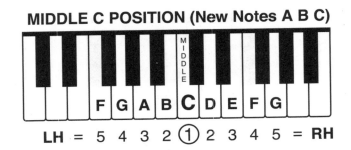

MIDDLE C POSITION (New Notes A B C)

The Quidditch World Cup

(from *Harry Potter and the Goblet of Fire*)

Music by Patrick Doyle
Arr. by Tom Gerou

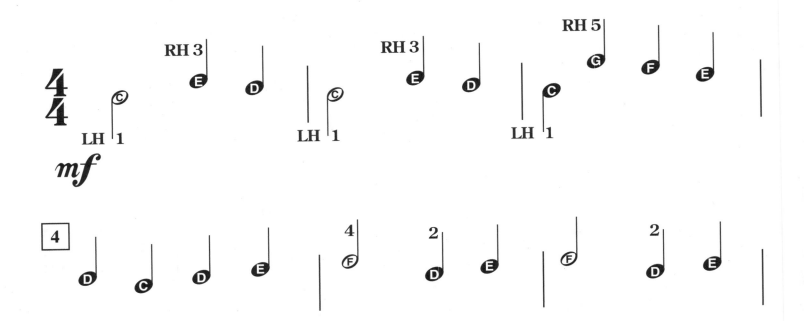

DUET PART (Student plays 1 octave higher.)

Moderately fast (in 2)

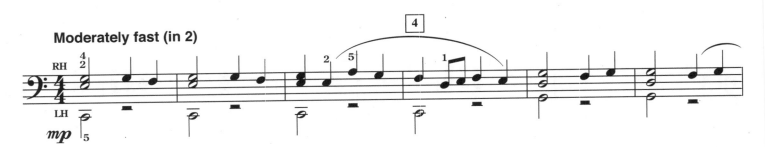

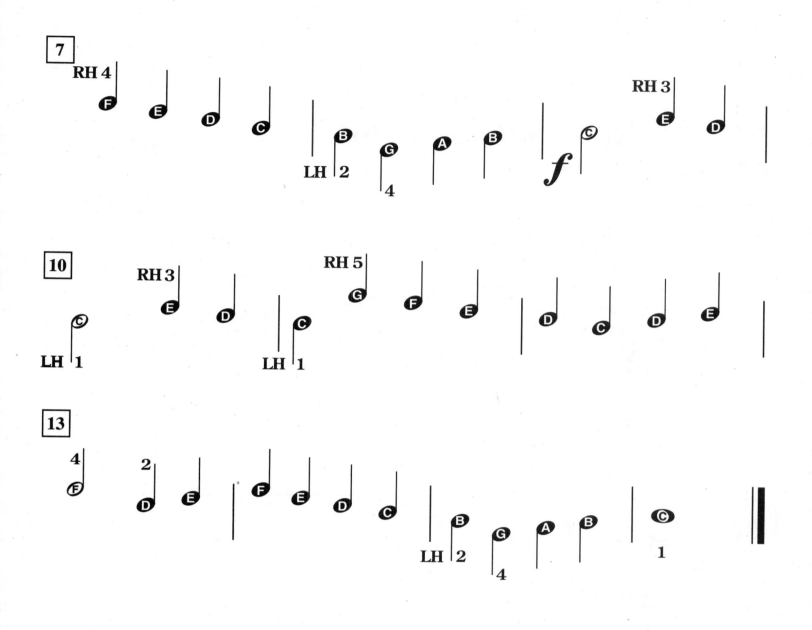

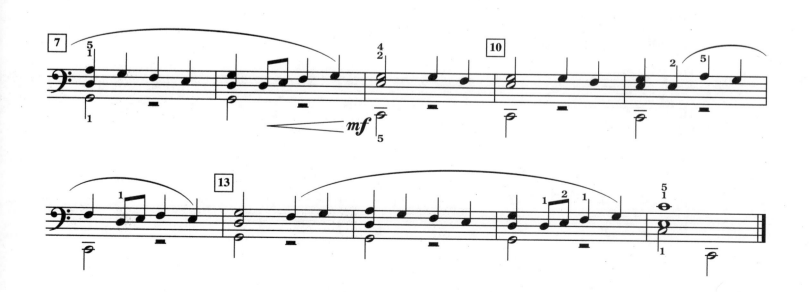

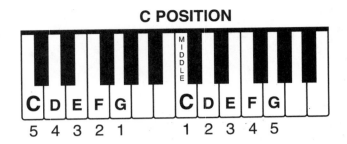

Wreck It, Wreck-It Ralph
(from Walt Disney's *Wreck-It Ralph*)

Music and Lyrics by Jamie Houston
Arr. by Tom Gerou

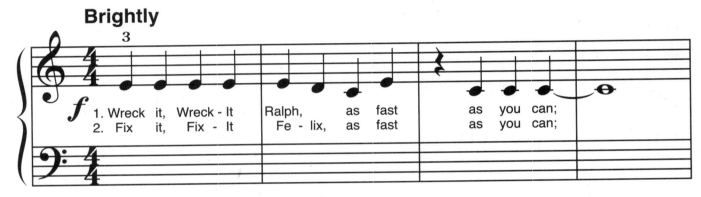

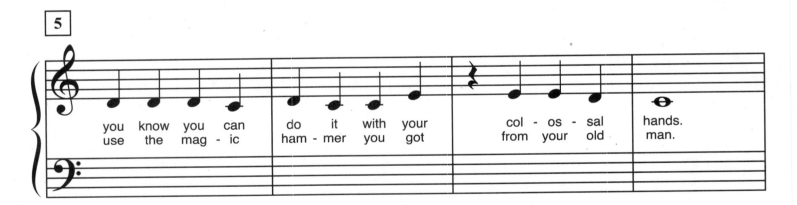

DUET PART (Student plays 1 octave higher.)

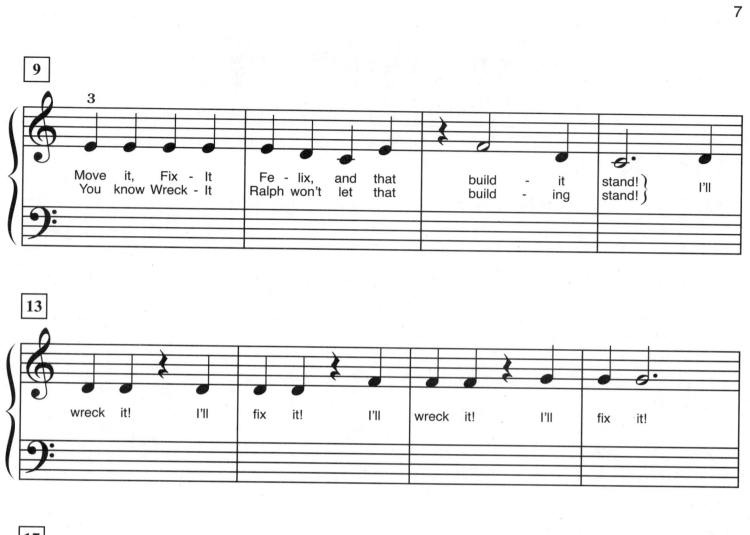

(You fixed it!)

Move it, Fix - It Fe - lix, and that build - it stand! I'll
You know Wreck - It Ralph won't let that build - ing stand!

wreck it! I'll fix it! I'll wreck it! I'll fix it!

Use after page 28.

C POSITION

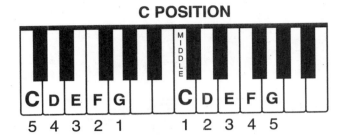

Cool Kids

Words and Music by
Graham Sierota, Jamie Sierota,
Noah Sierota, Sydney Sierota,
Jeffery Sierota and Jesiah Dzwonek
Arr. by Tom Gerou

Moderately fast

I wish that I could be like the cool kids,

'cause all the cool kids, they seem to fit in.

DUET PART (Student plays 1 octave higher.)

Moderately fast (in 2)

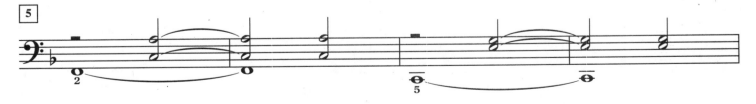

I wish that I could be like the cool kids,

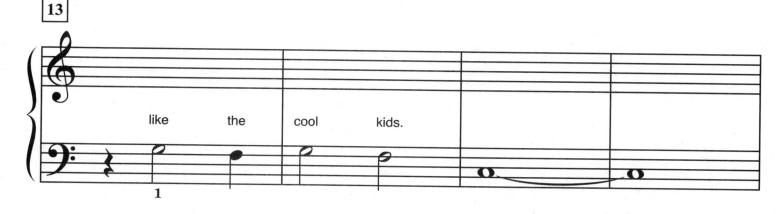

like the cool kids.

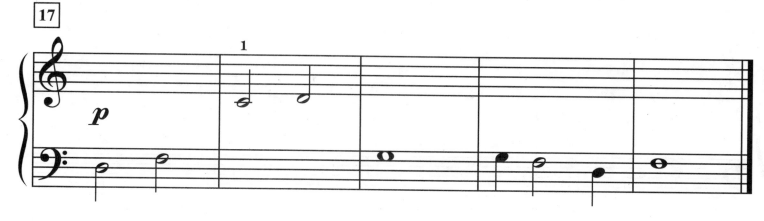

Use after page 29.

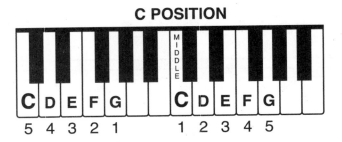

C POSITION

Just the Way You Are (Amazing)

Words and Music by Khalil Walton, Peter Hernandez,
Philip Lawrence, Ari Levine and Khari Cain
Arr. by Tom Gerou

Moderately fast

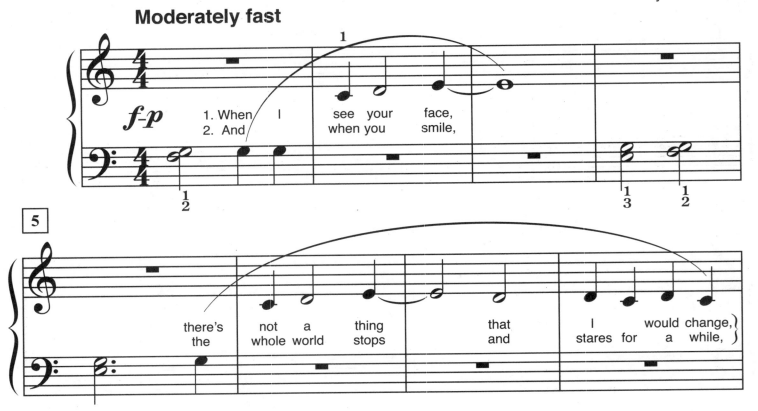

1. When I see your face,
2. And when you smile,

there's the
not a whole world thing stops
that and
I would change,
stares for a while,

DUET PART (Student plays 1 octave higher.)

Moderately fast (in 2)

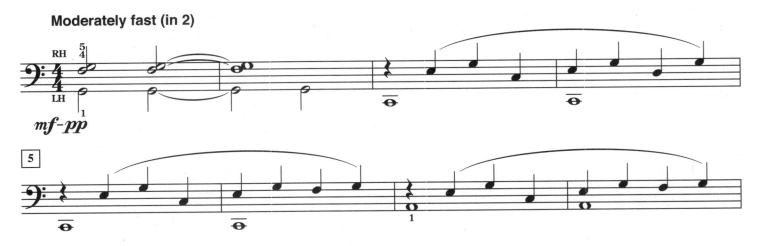

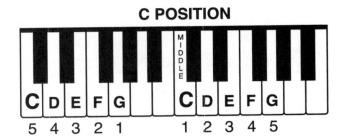

C POSITION

I'll Stand by You

Words and Music by Billy Steinberg,
Chrissie Hynde and Tom Kelly
Arr. by Tom Gerou

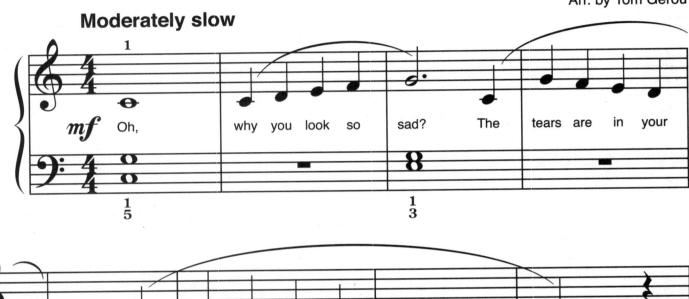

Moderately slow

Oh, why you look so sad? The tears are in your eyes. Come on and come to me now. And

DUET PART (Student plays 1 octave higher.)

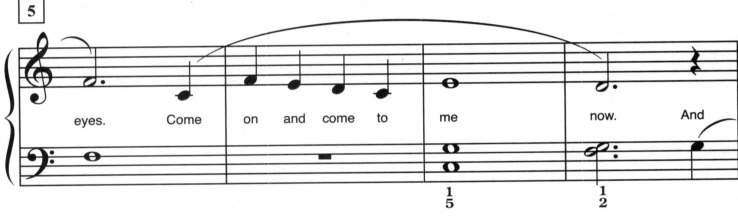

Moderately slow

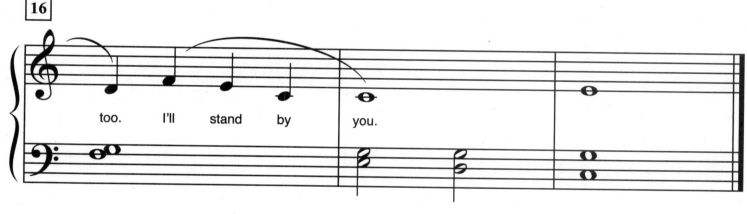

Theme from Superman

Music by **JOHN WILLIAMS**
Arr. by Tom Gerou

DUET PART (Student plays 1 octave higher.)

Chitty Chitty Bang Bang

Words and Music by
Richard M. Sherman and Robert B. Sherman
Arr. by Tom Gerou

Moderately fast

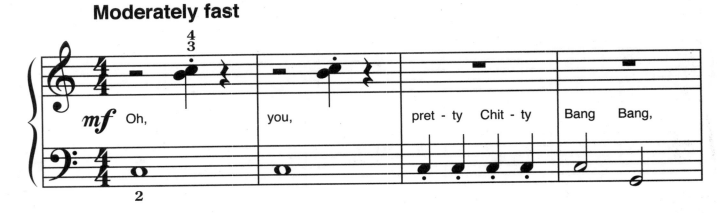

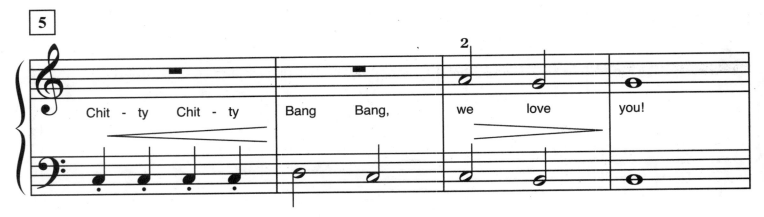

DUET PART (Student plays RH 1 octave higher, LH 2 octaves higher.)

Moderately fast (in 2)

Clouds

Words and Music by Zach Sobiech
Arr. by Tom Gerou

DUET PART (Student plays 1 octave higher.)

Use after page 44.

When Can I See You Again?

(from Walt Disney's *Wreck-It Ralph*)

Words and Music by Adam Young,
Matthew Thiessen, and Brian Lee
Arr. by Tom Gerou

Allegro moderato

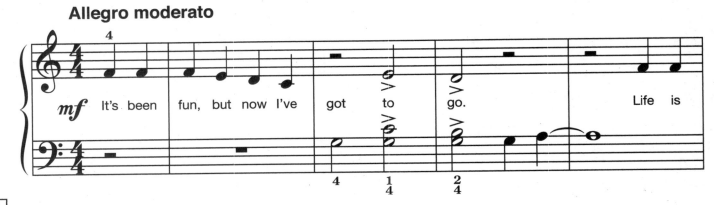

It's been fun, but now I've got to go. Life is

way too short to take it slow. But be - fore I go and

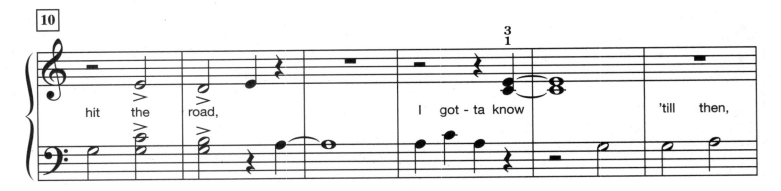

hit the road, I got - ta know 'till then,

DUET PART (Student plays 1 octave higher.)

Allegro moderato

Let It Go
(from Walt Disney's *Frozen*)

Music and Lyrics by
Kristen Anderson-Lopez and Robert Lopez
Arr. by Tom Gerou

DUET PART (Student plays 1 octave higher.)

Everything Is Awesome

(Awesome Remixx!!!)
(from *The LEGO Movie*)

Music by Shawn Patterson
Lyrics by Shawn Patterson, Andy Samberg,
Akiva Schaffer, Jorma Taccone,
Joshua Bartholomew and Lisa Harriton
Arr. by Tom Gerou

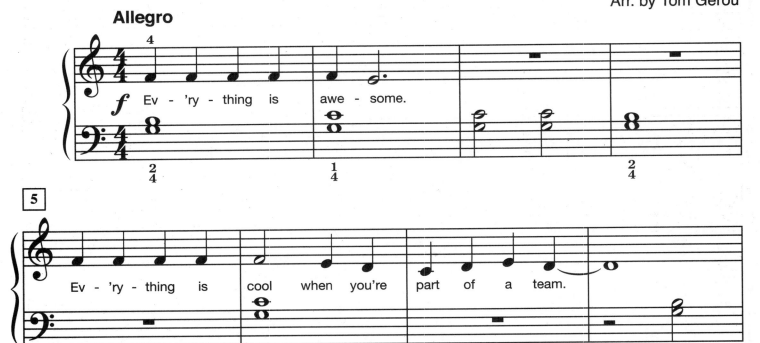

DUET PART (Student plays 1 octave higher.)

Moog City
(from *Minecraft*)

Composed by Daniel Rosenfeld
Arr. by Tom Gerou

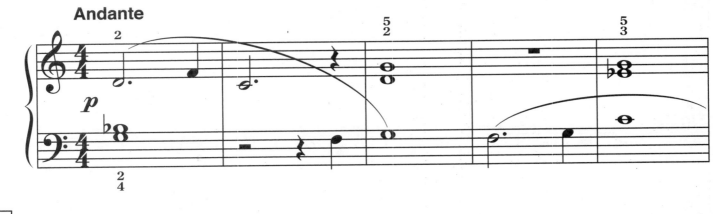

DUET PART (Student plays 2 octaves higher.)

Mamma Mia
(from *Mamma Mia!*)

Words and Music by Benny Andersson,
Stig Anderson and Bjorn Ulvaeus
Arr. by Tom Gerou

Yes, I've been bro - ken - heart - ed, blue since the day we part - ed.

Why, why, did I ev - er let you go? Mam-ma Mi - a,

now I real-ly know, my, my, I should not have let you go.

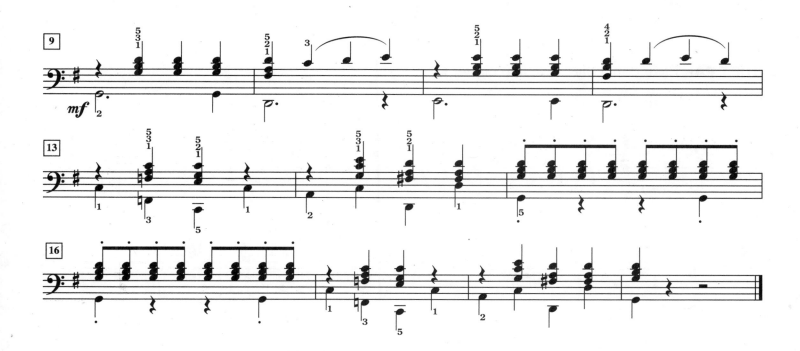

Cantina Band
(from *Star Wars Episode IV: A New Hope*)

Music by **JOHN WILLIAMS**

Arr. by Tom Gerou

Allegro

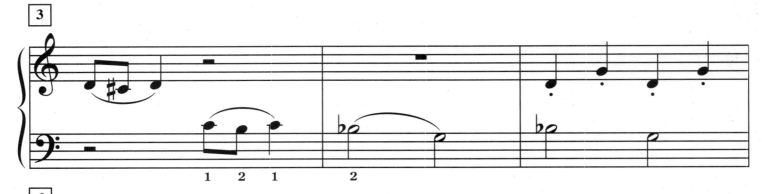

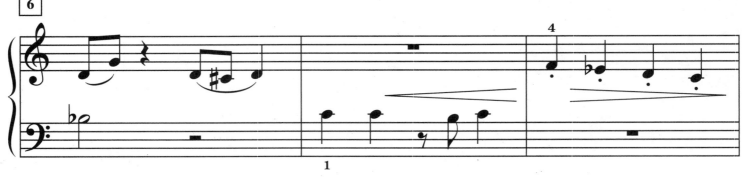

DUET PART (Student plays 1 octave higher.)

Allegro

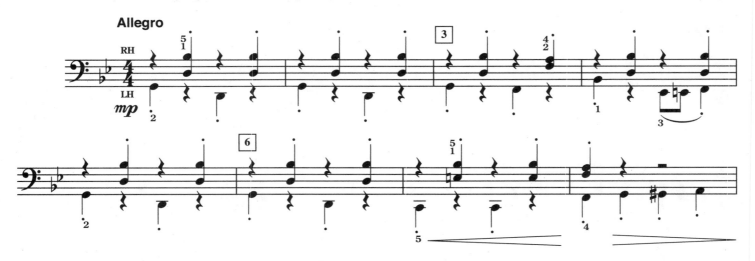

Believer

Words and Music by Zachary Barnett, James Adam Shelley,
Matthew Sanchez, David Rublin, Shep Goodman and Aaron Accetta

Arr. by Tom Gerou

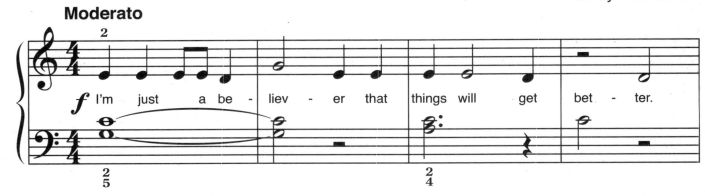

I'm just a be - liev - er that things will get bet - ter.

Some can take it or leave it, but I don't wan - na let it go!

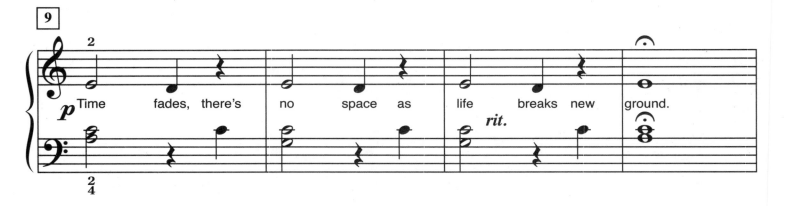

Time fades, there's no space as life breaks new ground.

DUET PART (Student plays 1 octave higher.)

Batman Theme

Words and Music by Neal Hefti
Arr. by Tom Gerou

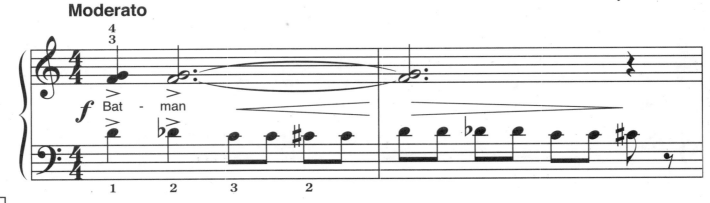

DUET PART (Student plays 1 octave higher.)

All About That Bass

Words and Music by
Meghan Trainor and Kevin Kadish

Arr. by Tom Gerou

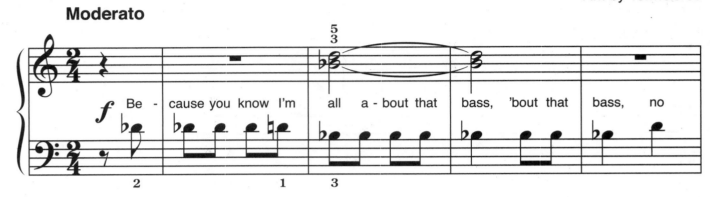

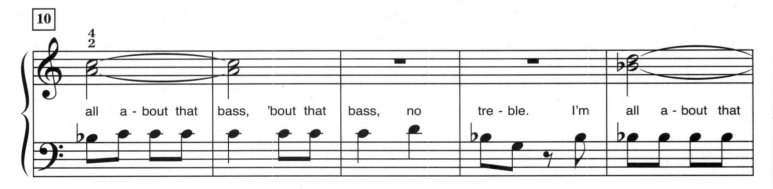

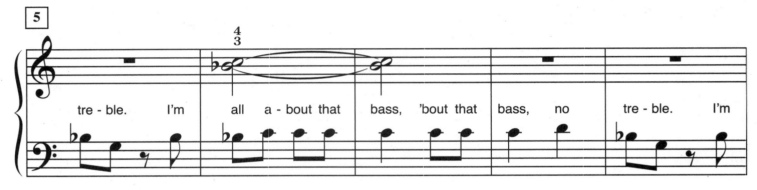

DUET PART (Student plays 1 octave higher.)

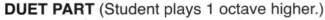

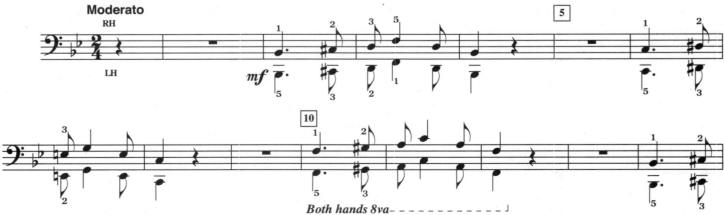

Both hands 8va- - - - - - - - - - - -

Use after pages 68–69.

Baby

Words and Music by
Terius Nash, Christopher Stewart, Christine Flores,
Christopher Bridges and Justin Bieber
Arr. by Tom Gerou

DUET PART (Student plays 1 octave higher.)

May the Force Be with You

(from *Star Wars Episode V: The Empire Strikes Back*)

Music by **JOHN WILLIAMS**
Arr. by Tom Gerou

DUET PART (Student plays 1 octave higher.)